Inain Barbara Assunção Americo

You just have to start learning!

Inain Barbara Assunção Americo

You just have to start learning!

Capoeira a great tool

ScienciaScripts

Imprint

Cover image: www.ingimage.com

This book is a translation from the original published under ISBN 978-3-639-74869-7.

Publisher:
Sciencia Scripts
is a trademark of
Dodo Books Indian Ocean Ltd. and OmniScriptum S.R.L publishing group

120 High Road, East Finchley, London, N2 9ED, United Kingdom
Str. Armeneasca 28/1, office 1, Chisinau MD-2012, Republic of Moldova, Europe
Managing Directors: Ieva Konstantinova, Victoria Ursu
info@omniscriptum.com

Printed at: see last page
ISBN: 978-620-8-60737-1

AUTHOR
INAIN BARBARA ASSUNÇÃO

THIS WORK HAS BEEN CARRIED OUT IN CURITIBA'S PRIVATE EDUCATION NETWORK FROM 1993 TO THE PRESENT DAY. IT IS A PROJECT TO ENCOURAGE BODILY EXPRESSION THROUGH BRAZILIAN CULTURE, USING CAPOEIRA AS ITS BASE.

BEGAN AS AN EXPERIMENT AND SPECIAL CLASS IN NURSERY SCHOOLS, WITH THE AIM OF DIVERSIFYING AND MAKING LEARNING MORE ATTRACTIVE.

THE WORK CARRIED OUT WITH COMMITMENT HAS BEEN SUCCESSFUL, HELPING TO IMPROVE THE QUALITY OF LIFE AND TEACHING IN THE PRE-SCHOOL PHASE, SUPPORTING EDUCATION PROFESSIONALS IN YET ANOTHER FORM OF LITERACY.

I'M A CHILD, ONE DAY I'LL GROW UP AND SHOW EVERYONE CAPOEIRA FOR REAL

I PLAY CAPOEIRA I PLAY MACULELE I SPEND THE MORNING PLAYING UNTIL DUSK, SAMBA, HAMMOCK PULLING, CAPOEIRA I LOVE YOU.

MY MUM ALWAYS USED TO SAY, MY SON, LET'S STUDY, THEN GO TO CAPOEIRA, I KNOW YOU'LL LIKE IT THERE, I'LL TAKE MY BERIMBAU, I JUST WANT TO PLAY.

YOU HAVE AN ENERGY THAT NO ONE CAN HOLD BACK BECAUSE WHEN YOU'RE A CHILD YOU HAVE TO PLAY, YOU'RE A CAPOEIRA, THE FUTURE OF ABADÁ.

(Author: AMAURI PEDROSO AMERICO- INSTRUTOR CABOCLO)

THIS BOOK WAS CREATED TO ADD TO THE KNOWLEDGE OF PRE-SCHOOL TEACHERS ANOTHER SUBSIDY FOR TEACHING THE MUCH-NEEDED LITERACY.

SUMMARY

Presentation

In describing this work, a paradigm shift is proposed to the educational method that is in evidence at school. This suggestion brings together Brazilian culture, the art of capoeira, and Gardner's multiple intelligences, whose vision is a differentiated pedagogical practice, with assistance for all difficulties, resolving them in the classroom before handing them over to another professional in another area.

Gardner contributes his theory to the teaching of capoeira as a guiding axis in the initial process of literacy when he mentions that people are different in their integrity so why not use different methods for each individual, with the teaching of capoeira to support literacy, you will understand the systematic study of body schema, laterality, balance, attention, concentration, space-time as a prerequisite for literacy.

In order for this experience to be successful in the classroom, it is necessary for the teacher to understand the systematisation of capoeira teaching so that they can make the correlation between body movement and alphabetic rhythm.

Capoeira, a genuinely Brazilian art, can contribute to the learning of various areas of knowledge without being imposed. Through its playfulness, history, maths, science and Portuguese will be easy to understand when you play with its concepts.

For children in early childhood education and in this age group, singing is very pleasurable and meaningful. The teacher can and should contextualise and comment on the song being sung, since capoeira singing is popular and usually tells a true story. Capoeira songs can be explored in language classes, for example, developing interdisciplinary work, which makes learning more meaningful, as we combine experience with reality.

Developing body skills as a facilitating element of everyday life will contribute to a significant increase in the initial phase of literacy, especially if educators, teachers, parents and the community are interacting with the teaching-learning process, giving it a broad re-significance.

(Photo of the game "Captain of the bush catches a slave.")

CHAPTER 1

Introduction

Through observations, it has been noted that educators find it very difficult to transform a non-literate class into a homogeneous literate class, realising the importance of the pre-school phase, which is often skipped due to lack of resources or even foolishness on the part of parents and family members.

The literacy teacher must be aware of the tough task of literacy, rescuing skipped stages such as the development of laterality, or notions of space-time, are things that the educator will have to propose to the students who need it, so why not do it in a playful way through capoeira.

Schools that have already adopted this art form as part of their curriculum say that they have seen good results in all aspects, but mainly because it contributes to Brazilian culture. Even schools with a foreign clientele choose to show our culture to other cultures.

In this book we will show you another methodology for literacy, in addition to the basic principles of capoeira, respecting traditional, constructivist and interactionist methods, and we will show you a unique method that includes all the others.

None of the movements covered in this book are intended to teach the teacher Capoeira techniques. To do so will require years of practical and theoretical study, and the purpose of this book is to show a new vision of teaching literacy.

(children in capoeira class exploring their movements)

"Kapu - eira in Tupi Guarani means sparse undergrowth and was considered a struggle by the **Bantu slaves in their desire for freedom"..., after many years the teaching of capoeira** has become increasingly methodical, schools that have innovative methodological proposals have adapted the teaching of capoeira over time.

Today Capoeira has transformed its teaching into a pedagogical basis for the metamorphosis study of literacy.

Teaching Capoeira to pre-schoolers is the best time. Children who have Capoeira in their curriculum with weekly classes from nursery school until they leave at level III will be able to become literate without much effort, even if the stimulation of the environment in which they are inserted is not as intense. However, it's important to emphasise that the teacher must be allied to the teacher.

capoeira, the teacher and the student, all enjoying a networked relationship, not a straight line:

- Regular classes are necessary;
- Specifying which movements will develop the student's biomechanics is important;
- The interaction with the teacher will bring security and reliability to both professionals;

By working together, the teacher will constantly link what is learnt in Capoeira with his or her daily life in the classroom, and then the Capoeirista teacher will be sure to contribute to literacy. Parents and educators will be able to get a quicker return on the literacy process compared to contemporary traditional methods.

CHAPTER 2

SUBJECT

Literacy

THEME

Capoeira as a guiding principle in the initial phase of the literacy process

But what is literacy? And what is capoeirising? How do we direct one to the other? Who does this work? Will capoeira act as a facilitator of literacy?

Literacy is a very important topic and is part of human life, because it is addressed every day incessantly regardless of age group, we need it every moment of our day and considering literacy is something that is built from birth and we interact with the environment and culture, we need to learn it.

Nowadays, there is a growing awareness of the literacy process as a whole, and the importance of developing broad bodily expression needs to be taken into account. As a result, schools are more concerned with pre-school education and its development in relation to the individual's entire motor behaviour. In this way, it will be possible to provide information about these students and get to know their bodily difficulties.

At school, capoeira work is carried out by a professional who informs and aims to promote bodily well-being based on values and respect between people, with the aim of helping children and their parents to visualise the positive side of bodily expressiveness.

Capoeira, a genuinely Brazilian art, combines movement, orality and rhythm, a mixture that is very important in the process of building reading and writing skills, facilitating literacy. This is just one of the ways in which this art can contribute to this process. We can also mention other benefits of learning about the history of Brazilian colonisation, the link with ancestors and the expansion of knowledge about their cultural identity.

Capoeira as a means of expression is an integral part of human development and is related to our culture, rescuing our Cultural Identity, so it is necessary to stimulate children's courage and curiosity. The proposal to develop this work in education came about by valuing Brazilian culture, knowing the importance of movement in the daily life of human beings, especially in early childhood education, so why not use this art that will bring us not only a healthy life, but also knowledge of the history experienced by the Brazilian people.

For all the work structured around learning capoeira, we attach great importance to theory and practice. In the initial phase of the literacy process, we work through playfulness, so that we can apply the movements in a way that is cohesive with what is really necessary to facilitate literacy in the classroom.

According to Gardner, individuals can develop 9 intelligences, which he called multiple intelligences: verbal-linguistic intelligence, logical-mathematical intelligence, interpersonal intelligence, intrapersonal intelligence, kinaesthetic intelligence, spatial intelligence, musical intelligence naturalistic intelligence, pictorial intelligence.

The kinaesthetic intelligence says that the individual assimilates his knowledge through the movements he performs, relating it to his learning, the musical intelligence shows us the significant learning through musicality, inter and intrapersonal, These are two intelligences that with the practice of capoeira we can internalise and relate better to ourselves and to others as a sign of mutual respect. In short, if each being is individual and what we find in question at school is teaching and learning, why not associate capoeira with the broad well-being of the individual and the quality teaching that is so expected by students, educators and parents.

According to Smolka 1993, "Attention is focussed on writing as a complicated motor skill to be developed and concerns **are focused on the "pre-requisites of literacy", based on the notions of "maturation" and the "acquisition of basic mechanisms" such as** motor coordination, laterality and others."

By developing body skills as a facilitating element for the cognitive process in various areas of knowledge, the student will stimulate themselves, because an exercise done to discover their own body will make it easier for them to unleash so many other discoveries. The practice of exercises that lead to expressiveness, whether bodily or orally, will help with the individual's cognitive aspect and will also help with respect for others, acting on the child's affective, social and political maturation, thus preparing them to exercise full citizenship.

CHAPTER 3

SPELLING OR SINGING, THE THING IS TO START

Literacy, according to the Aurélio Buarque de Holanda dictionary, is teaching how to read.

Smolka goes on to say

...Firstly because, for me, literacy implies reading and writing, which I see as a discursive moment. Secondly, because the acquisition process itself also takes place in a succession of discursive moments, of interlocution, of interaction.

But we know that the main role of education, beyond showing simple signs that give our lives meaning, is to structure the process that aims to develop the potential of the human being, to awaken the person's conscience according to the time and culture in which they live through writing, obtaining information to know how to reorganise or change behaviour and reformulate ideas, adapting to change.

In the pre-school phase, expressiveness plays a fundamental role in helping

cognitive development. As well as integrating students into their social environment, it helps them to recognise the cultural value of their country through playful activities, regardless of race, ethnicity, gender or creed. According to Borges in his book Physical Education for Preschoolers (p.37), the process of motor development is directly linked to movements and their expressiveness, which is described through signs.

Literacy provides the conditions for children to create their own concepts and values about humanity, seeking to improve human relationships in a critical and responsible way. However, for the scribbling process, the child already needs to be developing their projective relationships, among which the most important is the laterality relationship, through which the whole process of writing and language is understood.

Projective relationships can be worked on through capoeira from the age of 2 using psychomotor body stimulation. The ginga, considered the symbol of capoeira (a basic movement that imitates walking with open steps) will help children distinguish parallel from diagonal, and with other movements such as the au, (star), the tesourinha (supine position with lower limbs apart), children will begin to have notions of measures and angles.

(Work on spatial orientation through body stimulation)

Literacy is the process of systematic intervention in the cognitive area, one of the objectives of which is social well-being. Emilia Ferreiro says that the first form of writing is drawing, and the very young child transposes it through figures. With this definition, it's easy to see that spatial orientation is necessary for children from a very early age, helping them to understand their body schema. Drawing is defined by representations of shapes generally on a surface (Sumerian literacy), using lines, dots and spots, and is innate to human beings.

Thus, from the moment of conception, even before birth, the child already receives influences from the social environment, and is able to transpose their first words into the construction of the pictorial form of writing. From the parents' expectations and desires in relation to formal writing, the initial process of literacy takes shape. Here, capoeira is a complementary axis when the roda is formed and the child is limited to developing the game of capoeira in a single space.

The construction of literacy will take place throughout early childhood education and includes everything that the individual puts down on paper: their personal scribbles, drawings, symbols, signs, words, in short, all learning.

At home, the child receives the first stimuli for writing, gestures, touches, words and attitudes are all signs observed by the child from the uterine stage onwards. Therefore, the child learns about himself and the other from the bonds he establishes with the most significant people, initially in the family context, then in his group of friends, at school, in short, in various spaces of coexistence. Based on these relationships, she develops her psychomotor skills, perfecting her technique, which was initially unigraphic.

The school has an irreplaceable social function. It is one of the most important institutions in society at any level and every individual has the right to participate and receive education and instruction there.

School is becoming more important every day, as families are increasingly unable to take on education, even though parents are the main educators of their children, but nowadays parents work long hours and their children are left to teachers in schools or nurseries. It's up to the school to develop critical thinking, the ability to judge, behaviour, friendships, among other things, so that students are prepared for life.

For this reason, in addition to specific content, schools need to work on topics that improve the quality of life of their students. One of the necessary themes is multiculturalism, as it is part of human development.

An integral part of personality development, which can affect everything from literacy to school performance, is the lack of motor skills. Schools cannot ignore this dimension of the human being and must invest in body education, not in an athletic way, but in a way that develops biomechanics and cognition.

So why not adopt capoeira as a physical activity, providing children with cultural, artistic, historical and educational knowledge as well as motor development.

This guidance should take place on a collective level, promoting information and discussions that consider literacy in its biological and socio-cultural dimensions. The age range of the students must also be adapted to their needs and cognitive abilities.

In pre-school, the work takes place in an integrated way, with a lot of clarity and playfulness. In this way, literacy is built from the articulation with the formal environment and culture.

Therefore, the school's role in literacy is to broaden knowledge of the symbols linked to the signs that exist in society. With this, students can reflect and develop their line of reasoning without rushing to transpose the meanings.

The initial process of literacy is very complex according to Piaget, so we need to take a look at everything. We'll start by defining language, for (MICOTTI, 1987) **this is defined as a natural faculty and meaning is the counter-part of the auditory image, in other words, what the child assimilates.**

> "I'm a child, one day I'm going to grow up and show everyone capoeira for real (author Amauri Pedroso Americo - INSTRUTOR CABOCLO) (this would be the language that children record through repetition).

In this capoeira song, where gestures are an assimilative part of the song, if the child hugs itself, it is assimilating that the word child can be associated with it, which is why it hugs itself.

Thinking between the ages of 7 and 8 (the concrete operative phase) reaches a balance between assimilation and accommodation, forming the logical-mathematical and spatial-temporal group that is so important to the process. In this way, capoeira will provide the subject with the opportunity to new paths to reach the end without using a ready-made model, with its movements executed first from the whole and then from the parts, Piaget in Smolka,1997 tells us that when you teach the child something, you prevent them from making a discovery for themselves, while **Vigotsky, elaborating the concept of the "potential zone of development", states** that the child will do tomorrow alone what they do today in co-operation, which is why it is necessary for the child to have a vision of the whole and the accompaniment of professionals in order to be independent and proactive.

CHAPTER 4

HOW DO WE MAKE CAPOEIRA A LITERACY TOOL?

When a capoeira professional discovers himself in the educational environment, he makes this work a pleasure, classifies his classes, evaluates himself in order to give the content and his clients a good educational performance, so the capoeirista teacher can take this work in two ways: within the curriculum matrix, as a cross-curricular subject involving the areas of knowledge or as a special class, but both ways will have a duration of 30 minutes of activity for levels I, II and III per week.

Transversality proposes that both the concept of multiculturalism proposed in the PCN's and its objectives and contents for work be covered by the different areas of knowledge (disciplines). It's not a question of creating new content, but of unveiling the dimension of literacy in all areas of knowledge. Part of this work has already been carried out individually. The other part can be done by the teacher when planning their work with each item of content, making the capoeira dimension explicit as the guiding axis in the initial literacy process.

As we are proposing to work with pre-school children, we could start capoeira activities with nursery school children (2 year olds) and continue throughout the pre-school years.

From level I onwards, the work can be more systematised by providing a specific space. The effectiveness of capoeira's educational activities will be carried out in conjunction with the parents, and will be observed throughout the annual work, through workshops, weekly meetings and experiences, with the parents contributing to the elaboration of the information received on the cultural obstacles that hinder the acceptance of this cultural activity.

(Capoeira as a means of individual, family and social expression)

Valuing and appreciating the expressiveness experienced in capoeira will only have value if everyone participates. This will favour the socialisation of the child as a whole, whether in the school, family or social community. It will be by understanding the importance of movement in the individual's daily life that we will discover together the historical concepts experienced and used in capoeira.

Capoeira is the only genuinely Brazilian art to have developed the trilogy of song - rhythm - movement from its cradle and it is from the development of this psychomotricity that we will help these children to awaken their critical sense and their citizenship.

CHAPTER 5

READ OR PLAY, IT'S ALL ABOUT UNLOCKING

The importance of this process

Literacy is a formal process that begins in a broad context through the family and school environment and continues throughout life. In addition to the family, the media, science, customs and sometimes even the school interfere as barriers in this process. We see capoeira as a facilitating process for the systematic methodology of literacy that promotes reflection on expressiveness within Brazilian culture, such as: values, posture, attitudes, prejudices, experience and information.

Literacy is aimed at the well-being of individuals, favouring the experience of human beings with the environment in which they live in a pleasurable and responsible way. In order for capoeira professionals to understand that literacy adds signs to the student that will later make them understand the world in a holistic vision, it will be necessary to develop clear communication in interpersonal relationships, to develop their own values based on critical thinking, to understand the world around them and to make responsible decisions in all aspects of life.

This is where the Euclidean relationships come in, giving the child references of space and time. The teacher works capoeira with exercises where the other is **part of the "I" in a simultaneous exchange of partnerships, gingar dois a dois (one in** front of the other) um, esquiva (squatting) the other does the queixada (vertical posture making a semicircle outwards with one of the lower limbs) passing the leg over the esquiva, for example, **will provide the correlation of the letters "open" "closed" thus making their own cognitive structuring** in relation to the signs.

CHAPTER 6

WHAT ARE THOSE LYRICS?

One of the main points regarding literacy is the professional who will work on it and how the methodology will be applied.
So we asked...

Should the literacy teacher be a specialist in capoeira or in literacy?

Our aim here is to focus on the educator as a facilitator of the process, since his work will be pedagogical in nature, with the capoeirista himself providing the basis for the classroom teacher to achieve literacy, transmitting confidence for the student to master their corporeality in a global way.

Literacy work should begin with knowledge of the body's schema, notions of space-time, laterality, balance, rhythm, attention, respect for difficulties, so why not enhance the work of this Brazilian art? So educators interested in working in this context should always be in touch with theoretical issues, readings and discussions in a group space to supervise the work carried out.

Here we will give the group a very important role: it must always reflect so that there is a good theoretical basis for the capoeirista educator, giving him a foundation for the work that will be developed, which will help him in the classroom later on, but it will be the educator's role to be able to clarify doubts, treating naturally all the issues that may remain unresolved after the pedagogical meetings involving capoeira.Always respecting each other's opinions, creating opportunities to broaden the students' and their parents' vision of capoeira and their real need for accompaniment in the literacy process at an early stage is its greatest importance, showing improvement in cognitive learning performance with the adjustments made by capoeira in the psychomotor part.

The aim is for participants to be able to question history (for example, who the slaves were; the captain of the bush; Princess Isabel), rethink values (since the capoeira roda makes it possible to integrate the most diverse social classes without the need for formal presentations) by involving participants (regardless of their race or ethnicity) and develop greater sensory skills that will enable them to mature autonomously in relation to their friends. For this to happen, it is necessary for the educator and the institution's pedagogical team to be aware of the legal, biological, cultural, religious and political aspects present in society when approaching capoeira x literacy.

The subject of capoeira is still very controversial among Aryan classes, so the aim is to help students reflect on what is already part of their concerns: race and ethnicity. The role of the school here is of paramount importance, mediating the internal survival of the students by establishing rules of coexistence, thus clarifying inclusion in a broad and holistic way in the public but educational space.

The community needs to internalise that inclusion doesn't just refer to people with special needs, but also to anyone who differs from the standardised model of elitist society. Learning to live with differences means learning to discriminate between public and private spaces. Presenting issues in a democratic way, in a climate of trust and respect, will only contribute to this innovative work, adding notions of citizenship to the students from an early age and into their lives.

CHAPTER 7

MY MATERIAL

What I use in class

The capoeirista teacher can use a variety of materials including pedagogical strings, alternative pandeiros, berimbaus, atabaque chicotinho, larger strings, always contributing to literacy, we can start at this point in the work, as everyone will enjoy exploring the materials, it will be necessary for the educator to ask for everyone's help at the end of the work to organise the materials, reporting what was done in class is also a good discursive resource for a self-evaluation of the educational process.

This professional can also contribute to literacy by organising the ideas of a capoeira song used in class on a piece of paper, the text memorises and documents something useful for capoeira classes, as well as helping you to tidy up the materials used in class.

Smolka, 1993 - A text is a way of organising ideas. It is a work that is carried out. It is the constitution of memory, documentation, history, because it makes it possible to distance oneself and return, it makes it possible to read? (Not one! Several!)

In this way, the educator must be made aware of the difficult task of teaching, and not be a victim of the process as a whole. Therefore, the professional who will be working with capoeira as the guiding axis of literacy must be reinforced by the entire pedagogical team of the institutions and, in fact, will be committed to teaching and learning, all through their world view and their records, their texts.

Transmitting confidence, taking into account the needs of each student and establishing relationships between capoeira and the basics in the early stages of literacy will only favour the capacity for bodily self-knowledge, when the student problematises issues related to the various areas of knowledge on their own.

will only be making their knowledge interdisciplinary, a possibility that capoeira will provide throughout their learning.

But we mustn't forget that when dealing with this systematised space, be it the classroom or the sports field, the street where you live or the pavement, we will have to order the body notions we have acquired, such as: front, back, up, down, and the educator must respect the various stages of psychomotor development that the children have reached so far, and from this knowledge the professional will begin their work on building new body aids. To do this, they must adopt an ethical approach to their work, respecting the difficulties of **themselves and others, and always respecting the normative attitudes of "right and wrong", "normal and pathological".**

It should be emphasised here that everyone receives some kind of bodily education that is influenced by their cultural context. In Brazil, the patriarchal, macho culture is still predominant, and boys are forbidden to roll over, fall down, cry, etc. Capoeira has an important role to play in breaking down this paradigm, making prejudice, discrimination and social exclusion impossible.

CAPOEIRA MUSIC

"The boy cried"

Nhé, Nhé, Nhé

Because you didn't suck

Nhé, Nhé, Nhé...(Public domain)

We know that the first social exclusion that an individual goes through is not knowing how to read, let's look at a package leaflet where the medicine is not yet known to us and will only be made clear to us when we read the leaflet, among many other examples that we could cite, children's curiosity and their first questions about what is written there or there could be called topological relationships, in other words, those that are elementary and that don't distinguish any geometric shape, let alone signs. For capoeira, these questions are significant, because in this way the children will relate to **the knowledge of their origin ("why am I white or black?"; "why am**

I bigger or smaller?") and the desire to know, to learn. Satisfying these curiosities generates new interests and knowledge, which capoeira can fulfil with its **history, which is called "our culture".** So as not to interfere with formal learning, the educator will pass on Brazilian culture through playfulness.

"According to Freitas, p. 41, 1997 - In addition to working on temporal and spatial perception, initiative and decision-making, key elements of history are recalled**, and passed on through play."**

The choice of game can be related to the classroom content, reinforcing what is being proposed in a playful and delicious way

(In this game called capitão do mato pega escravo, tell the children who these figures from our history were, why the slave ran away and the importance of their union for survival).

CHAPTER 8

WHICH IS THE BEST SCHOOL?

How to choose my child's school

By choosing a school, a formal space for building knowledge, parents and children experience new ways of relating, getting to know each other and establishing emotional bonds.

At school, the desire to know, discover, learn and teach circulates. We educators are always learning and re-learning, each year a new class and each generation is different, the world changes, young people change and we are challenged in what we knew or thought we knew, so why not start by telling our students that each letter has a function and distinguish with them its codification, decoding and its sign, as is done in capoeira, to each incoming student we give them a nickname that will differentiate and distinguish them from the others, but it is important that this is a playful form and above all of acceptance by the child, only then will the nickname become a pedagogical and playful form, bringing to the children a new form of integration and respect for others for what they choose.

School, like life, is a place of diversity in terms of gender, ethnicity, age, belief, social class... Mutual respect is therefore needed between educators and children, so that everyone feels recognised and welcomed in their different life stories. (FERREIRO, 1992) says that the way in which writing is represented provides an understanding of social functions and their objectives (books, newspapers, packaging, medicines, posters, etc.) for someone who doesn't codify any of these mentioned in their different life stories will be someone with no future prospects, so it's up to us to provide a little joy and enchantment to these little ones who come to us, always stimulating and encouraging.

Parental support when choosing a school is super important, as well as knowing its curriculum and methodologies. Capoeira shouldn't be hidden in the middle of the school's special tasks, since it will be the school that publicises our culture.

It is therefore suggested that the school offer a space for chats, where parents can find out about the objectives, contents and procedures of both the classroom and capoeira classes, and clarify any doubts that may arise about capoeira's work as an axis of literacy. Some parents may not agree with the work of capoeira because they feel insecure about their creed or belief because they don't know the real importance and true meaning of the objectives set by the work, some even abhor the idea that capoeira will re-educate their children religiously, it is up to the educator together with the pedagogical coordination to explain all the educational development of capoeira in the school, and the real meaning of this Brazilian culture.

Of course, it's not up to the school to dictate standards, to say what is "moral or immoral", but to talk to the community and put it into context. This can be done with clear, simple and direct communication, and can include a brief experience of what will be transmitted during the lessons. In these meetings, the basic principles of capoeira should be laid out, such as: the stance that the educator will adopt when approaching literacy with the students; respect for differences of creed - colour - race - ethnicity; body recognition associated with the responsibility of literacy; and the right of everyone to exercise their citizenship in a unique way.

The support of the school's management, supervision and pedagogical coordination is fundamental to guaranteeing better infrastructural conditions and the participation of the school community. Breaking paradigms dictated by the traditionalists of educational history guarantees commitment and innovation in education.

the approach to capoeira at school is recommended by the MEC through the PCN'S when it talks about multicultural and interdisciplinary work.

The school can make a huge contribution to the education of its pupils by making room for the plurality of conceptions, values and beliefs that pupils can express, respecting each other's opinions and differences and thus intervening in situations where children and adolescents' rights are violated in order to ensure their physical and moral integrity.

CHAPTER 9

CHILDREN'S CORPOREALITY

SEXUAL EXPRESSION

Schools are usually approached by a significant number of parents who ask for advice on how to behave with their children when they are faced with the first child sexual manifestations or when they are taken by surprise with questions about sexuality. Distressed, confused and embarrassed, they run to what they think is their immediate help - the teachers.

Another important role of capoeira is that it works on body contact from the very first lessons. It can also help children in an educational way, preparing them a little more for their first knowledge of the body and its transformations. It can even ease parents' discomfort about children's sexuality, not that the educator will deal with this subject intensely, but because he is the discoverer of body and facial expressiveness, he will also have the facility to show the differences between boys and girls in a playful and relaxed way, demystifying the taboos imposed by society.

The educator will not honestly lie to the child or tell **fanciful stories, such as the "stork" or the "little seed", but will respect the** child's age and ability to understand. Ideally - in simple, objective and clear language - **the educator will tell the child exactly "what" is different and "why" there is a difference, trying to answer only what the** child asks and not anticipate unnecessary information at the time.

One of the first questions that arises in the context of sexual curiosity around the age of four or five concerns human reproduction. "How was I born?", "How are babies born?" are the most commonly asked questions. When the child comes up with these questions, the educator (whether parents or teachers) should already have a previously formed answer, so it's interesting to start the explanation from the knowledge the child already has, trying to complete or correct the information. Leaving the subject until later or suppressing interest won't add anything to the child's knowledge, it will just add to it.

curiosity and further questions will arise. The best thing to do is to clarify and respond to curiosity, avoiding often erroneous and distorted information on the subject.

With regard to sexual manifestations, most teachers are horrified when they see their pupils touching their genitals or handling their own faeces and end up reinforcing the child's behaviour in an overwhelmed way. Such attitudes are harmful and can lead to conflictual situations in the sexual sphere.

If this happens during capoeira classes, the educator who is part of this discovery together with the child must understand their bodily manifestations, not in a conniving way, but by taking the child out of the situation they are in without attacking their morals or alarming their attitudes, since these are part of the child's interest in discovering the world and their own body, the magnificence of capoeira.

Body expression when working with inanimate objects gives children fantasies, which according to Vygotsky is linked to their zone of proximal development and directly to learning in process, so the best thing to do is to replace reprimands with frank conversations and attitudes that seek to divert the child's attention to other stimuli and activities, so as not to jeopardise children's development and creativity.

Repressing it will only alienate the child from their genitals, as they are associated with the idea **that they are "dirty, disgusting, ugly and forbidden".** Such beliefs can persist throughout life, influencing and even jeopardising the quality of future sexual life, something that slaves experienced when they arrived in Brazil with their unknown culture and which would later give rise to capoeira.

Finally, here is another area of basic education in which capoeira will help with psychological and sexual development in early childhood education. Using pandeiros made from alternative materials, the teacher will be able to give the children bodily activities that work on sexuality in a natural way without directly implicating the subject, providing the opportunity for discoveries that are so necessary for children.

CHAPTER 10

WHAT THE MASTER SAYS

LITERACY ACCORDING TO PIAGET

According to Piaget, the cognitive process is divided into four distinct but inseparable phases:

- Motor sensory (0 to 2 years)
- Pre-operative (2 to 4 years)
- Concrete operative (4 to 7 years)
- Formal Operative (from 7 years old)

These phases are determined by a systematic evolution in which, according to Piaget, error is necessary for the child to learn and make relationships establishing the phases of writing.

The classification also proposed by Piaget, an important factor for literacy, will be seen in the ground movements (bridge, fall on all fours with the back facing downwards or upwards) and in the basic movements (ginga and dodge). As for seriation, both literacy and capoeira go through 3 stages, 1ª stage - the child will organise class time, always knowing that they will have a warm-up - main part (roda) - return to calm, 2ª stage - the child will organise class time in a general way and won't be able to add a game without undoing the traditional organisation, and in the 3ª stage the child will internalise the whole class, even if the dynamics are different. Classification and sorting are important groupings for the transposition of signs.

According to Piaget, children up to the age of 2 or so don't have the ability to copy. Let's see: - When a **child writes scribbles** "////////##" they are in the unigraphic phase, that is, they are processing the informal writing that they understand (phase 0 to 2 years). Through the movements of capoeira in an expressive way, children will bring to the next phase of writing their knowledge of body schema, auditory perception and accentuated rhythm, giving them the required motor coordination and attention needed for the act of writing. It is at the age of 3 that the child begins to make scribbles, from 3 and a half to 4 years that the child really begins to draw with topological indications. The second stage is the syllabic-alphabetic stage, which is described by the drawing of ready-made signs but without decoding anything, e.g. a f t d, for the child recognises the letters and fancifully forms a word (stage 2 to 4 years).

This is where capoeira helps the child to develop laterality, balance, spatial orientation, visual perception, fine motor coordination and a better understanding of the signs. In normal development, the child already recognises the signs and their names. Until the age of 4, the child joins the capoeira circle and just executes the movements without differentiating the rhythm (slow or fast), just like in literacy, where the child doesn't obey the order of placement, only their similarities.

And it is from the age of 5 to 6 that the child will define curvilinear and rectilinear shapes, defining the transposed symbols in a more defined way, here too the child begins to reproduce the movements in capoeira classes according to the sound of the instruments (fast rhythm - fast movement, slow rhythm - slow movement).

The concrete operative phase in which Piaget reports that the child is able to imagine through what the other person reports is in the writing called pre-syllabic phase, here the instruments of capoeira (rhythm), its musicality (singing) and continuous movements are of paramount importance,

When you teach a child to play the pandeiro, for example, they will **separate the syllables of "pa pum pa pum"** with their mouths, training their orality, a necessary tool for literacy; the continuous movements of capoeira, as well as rhythmic notions, will provide the child with the cadence of writing in a playful way; and last but not least, the gesticulated singing of capoeira, as well as teaching the child in a contextualised way, will symbolise their main means of communication, orality and the meaning of language. In the latency phase (6 to 10 years), the child is very interested in learning new activities, making friends and writing. In writing, we call this stage alphabetic, the child is already writing formally with minimal errors and we have already managed to decode their writing, ending the work of capoeira as the guiding axis of literacy in the initial process and starting another stage of learning with this genuinely Brazilian culture.

CHAPTER 11

RESPECT AND PLAN

Effective work

When thinking about body classes, the ideal is not to work with a closed programme, as there is nothing to stop the teacher from adding exercises with broad approaches to psychomotor development, as long as they are related to the students' interests. However, it is of the utmost importance that the teacher has planned what he or she is going to work on based on the knowledge already established in other lessons, making it more productive in relation to the expectations related to literacy.

Here's an example of a lesson that could take place at three different times:

- Warming up (there may be a game or not), it will be through this that, jumping like popcorn or holding their feet to learn how to dodge (squatting movement) or holding their partner's hand while performing another movement, giving a brief notion of what the ginga will be like, the child will be perceiving their body and forming in their mind the knowledge of body schema.

- Main part (here the educator will go through the movements and the capoeira circle which will add conditioning for psychomotor development) - back to calm (here using a capoeira song added to an instrument and an exercise that relaxes the body, which has been the object of work all along).

- To finish off, the teacher could have everyone lie down and play a berimbau to facilitate relaxation. The counsellor could use games that help the student to introduce themselves with their nickname, defining the end of the lesson (identifying themselves by shouting, miming)...

The MEC and capoeira. Capoeira also educates.

Currently, pedagogues, sociologists and researchers in the field of education are almost unanimous in stating that the critical education of a people cannot be detached from its socio-cultural context, nor from its present reality.

(...)

The participation of popular culture in curricular content is taking on more and more dimensions. Certainly, there is an urgent need to open a gap in the curriculum for those who make up the culture of the real man, the popular man, the one who lives the day-to-day social conflicts, the one who has been resisting from generation to generation the excesses of the great figures and the heinous politicians.

And capoeira is there, with all its exuberant wealth of information, its symbolic richness, its movements of resistance that clearly denote our conflicted political trajectory, impregnated with abuses of power and domination.

Capoeira is also about body movement, music, improvisation, art, dance, freedom, class struggle, in short, in a capoeira roda, or any other activity inherent to its practice, you'll find all of these.

elements that are certainly part of everyone's daily life, which, if explored effectively and coherently, will obviously contribute to the instruction and education of our children, adolescents and adults. (...).

BIBLIOGRAPHICAL REFERENCES

AREIAS, A. das. What is capoeira? **São Paulo: Brasiliense, 1983.**

AZEVEDO, F. de. Brazilian culture. **São Paulo: Melhoramentos. 3ª edition, 1958.**

BONOW, Ivã Waisberg (translation). The world of the child - **in fifteen volumes. Rio de Janeiro: Delta S. A., 1931.**

BORGES, Célio José. Physical education in pre-school. **Rio de Janeiro: Sprint, 1987.**

CAMPOS, H. Capoeira na Escola. **Salvador: Presscolor, 1990.**

CORDEIRO, Y.C. Capoeira and self-esteem. **Brasília, 1998.**

ELIAS, Marisa D. De Emílio para Emília - **A trajectória da alfabetização. São Paulo, Editora Scipione, 2000.**

FERREIRA, Aurélio Buarque de Holanda. Minidicionário da língua portuguesa. **Rio de Janeiro: Nova Fronteira, 1977.**

FERREIRO, E. Reflexões sobre a alfabetização **São Paulo: cortez/ autores associados, 1985.**

FREITAS, Jorge Luiz de. Capoeira infantil: **a arte de brincar com o próprio corpo. Curitiba: Expoente, 1997.**

FREITAS, Jorge Luiz de. Capoeira infantil: **jogos e brincadeiras. Curitiba: Torre de papel, 2003.**

KOHL, Maryann F., SOLGA Kim. Discovering great artists: **art practice for children. Porto Alegre: Artmed, 2001.**

LURIA, ° R. The development of writing in children.

MEC.INEP.Alfabetização e Capoeira, Jornal do professor de 1° grau, Brasília- DF, September 1986, booklet, p.08

MICOTTI, M. C. de ° Piaget and the literacy process. **São Paulo 2ª ed. Editora pioneira, 1987.**

MOURA, ° de Os centros **de** interesse na escola: **2nd ed, São Paulo ed melhoramentos, 1931.**

PIAGET, J. The birth of intelligence in the child. **Rio de Janeiro: ed. Zahar, 1970.**

PIAGET, J. and INHELDER B. The Psychology of the Child. **Rio de Janeiro: ed. Bertrand Brasil, 1999.**

PIAGET, J. and INHELDER B. The Representation of Space in the Child. **Porto Alegre: Artes Medicas, 1993.**

SANTOS, Gláurea B. dos and SIMÕES, Sueli P. The literacy process - **Subsidies for efficient work. São Paulo: 10th edition Ática, 1997.**

SCHULTE, M.R.H. Desenrolando o Carretel: Vida de Professora. **São Paulo: ed. Articulada, 1996.**

SLAVIERO, Vânia Lúcia. Getting on with life at school: body-mind relaxation and emotions in the classroom. São Paulo: Ground publishing house, 2004.

SMOLKA, Ana Luiza B.. The child in the initial phase of writing. **São Paulo: Cortez Publishing House, 1993.**

SOUZA, Iracy de Sá. Psicologia **-A aprendizagem e seus problemas. Rio de Janeiro: Livraria José Olympio Editora S/A, 1969.**

SPODEK, B. and SARACHO, °N. Teaching children from three to eight years old. Rio de Janeiro

VIEIRA, Luiz Renato. The game of capoeira. **Rio de Janeiro: Sprint, 1995.**

VYGOTSKY, L.S. et al Language, development and learning, **2ªed., São Paulo ed. Ícone/Edusp, 1988.**

Text by : MARQUES, Marcelo Santos. The construction of children's space **(from primary school to 4th grade)**

Revista escola nova,April/1997 year XII - multiple intelligences - how this new theory is applied in maths teaching by a São Paulo school

ACKNOWLEDGEMENT

How much suffering, but it was worth it, nights worrying about whether what I really think is worth the fruits of the sacrifice, so...

Reading and studying, studying and reading to show everyone that Brazilian culture should be included in the educational curriculum as a means of formal education. The sleepless nights and the anguish over unread books were worth it , but it wouldn't have been any use if no one had encouraged me, so thank you.

I am immensely grateful to everyone who was involved in this arduous process of building this work, but I am eternally grateful to my mother Maria Sueli and my husband Amauri who often **played the role of "mum" to** my sons Leonardo and Nicolas, my two wonderful sons who, although they missed me, understood my absence and at no time did these four very important characters in my story make me give up.

I would like to thank the people who, even without realising it, helped to complete this project, my comadres Maria Trindade and Luciana Néri, more than comadres? Sisters, people who indirectly bore a heavy burden that wasn't theirs.

No less important is my master Camisa (José Tadeu), who was a great encouragement whenever I asked.

I'll end by thanking the almighty father who guided my thoughts to break yet another educational paradigm that our genuinely Brazilian culture, capoeira, is something for black people, slaves and bandits.

FIELD RESEARCH WITH THE INTERVIEW INSTRUMENT TO ADD MORE KNOWLEDGE TO THIS WORK.

I AM INAIN BARBARA ASSUNÇÃO AMERICO, I am here to enrich my research work, which is scientific in nature, thank you in advance for your collaboration.

CONTACT: barbaraabada@yahoo.com.br

1) Name of interviewee, profession and current area of work:

2) What do you think literacy is?

3) What do you see as the literacy process?

4) What does capoeira add to the educational environment?

5) For you, is the capoeira educator a facilitator in the initial literacy process?

6) What role should this professional play in the teaching-learning relationship?

7) How can capoeira professionals contribute to the early literacy process?

8) Do you believe that working with capoeira in Early Childhood Education will facilitate the literacy process in the early stages?

MIX
Papier aus verantwortungsvollen Quellen
Paper from responsible sources
FSC® C105338

Printed by Books on Demand GmbH, Norderstedt / Germany